Water in Our World

Cleaning Water

by Rebecca Olien

CAPSTONE PRESS
a capstone imprint

First Facts are published by Capstone Press,
1710 Roe Crest Drive, North Mankato, Minnesota 56003
www.capstonepub.com

Library of Congress Cataloging-in-Publication Data
Olien, Rebecca, author.
  Cleaning water / by Rebecca Olien. — [New edition]
     pages cm. — (First facts. Water in our world)
  Summary: "Describes how cities treat freshwater so that it is safe to drink"—Provided by publisher.
  Audience: Ages 7-9
  Audience: K to grade 3
  Includes bibliographical references and index.
ISBN 978-1-4914-8278-0 (library binding)
ISBN 978-1-4914-8282-7 (paperback)
ISBN 978-1-4914-8286-5 (eBook PDF)
1. Water—Purification—Juvenile literature. 2. Water-supply—Juvenile literature. I. Title.
  TD430.O42 2016
  628.1'62—dc23
                              2015026115

Editorial Credits
Abby Colich, editor; Kyle Grenz, designer; Wanda Winch, media researcher; Laura Manthe, production specialist

Photo Credits
Capstone, 16-17; Dreamstime: Luckydoor, 13, Izanbar, 10, Nostal6ie, 1, Presse750, 19; Shutterstock: AuntSpray, 7, Chaiyapruk Chanwatthana, 9, 15, daizuxion, 20, Ecelop, wave design, Kekyalyayan, cover, 1, KPG Payless2, 5, tachygossus, splash design

Table of Contents

To the Faucet

Turn on the faucet and clear, clean water rushes out. People drink millions of glasses of clean water each day. Getting clean water to the faucet is a long process. Water goes through many stages of cleaning before people can drink it.

Water Sources

The water people drink comes from different sources. In many areas people get water from rivers and lakes.

Some water seeps into the ground. It collects in underground *aquifers.* In some places people dig wells to reach *groundwater.*

aquifer—an underground lake
groundwater—water that is found underground

toxin—poison
filter—a device that cleans liquids or gases as they pass through it

7

Most water in rivers and lakes is not safe for people to drink. Rain washes dirt and waste into rivers. Waste from homes and farms *pollute* water sources.

Water treatment plants clean water to make it safe to drink. Dirt and other *particles* are taken out of the water. *Bacteria* that could make people sick are killed.

pollute—to make something dirty or unsafe
water treatment plant—a place where water is cleaned for people to use at home
particle—a tiny piece of something
bacteria—very small living things; some bacteria cause disease

Before water is treated, it must be pumped from a lake or river. Pumps also bring water up from under the ground.

Pumps push water through miles of large pipes. The pipes carry water to tanks in water treatment plants.

Fact!

In some places, *reservoirs* are created to store drinking water. The water is cleaned and moved to buildings from the reservoir.

reservoir—an artificial lake where water is collected

Water treatment plants take out *sediment*. Sediment is made up of dirt and particles found in water. A powder called alum is added to water. Alum makes the particles sticky. The sticky particles sink to the bottom of the tanks. Cleaner water is left on top. This water then is pushed through filters to take out any remaining particles.

sediment—bits of sand or clay carried by water or wind

This machine is removing sediment from water.

Disinfection

Disinfection is the next step in making water clean. Treatment plants disinfect water by adding *chemicals* that kill bacteria.

Most treatment plants add chlorine or chloramine to water. Treating water with these chemicals helps protect people from disease.

disinfection—a process that kills harmful germs
chemical—a substance that creates a reaction; chlorine is a chemical used to treat water

In this area of a treatment plant, chemicals are added to water.

Moving Water

Once it is treated, water is ready for people to use. Clean water is pumped from the treatment plant to storage tanks. Some cities and towns store water in large towers.

Cleaning Water

Source Water

Water is pumped to the treatment plant.

Removing Sediment

Alum is added. Sediment sinks to the bottom of the tank.

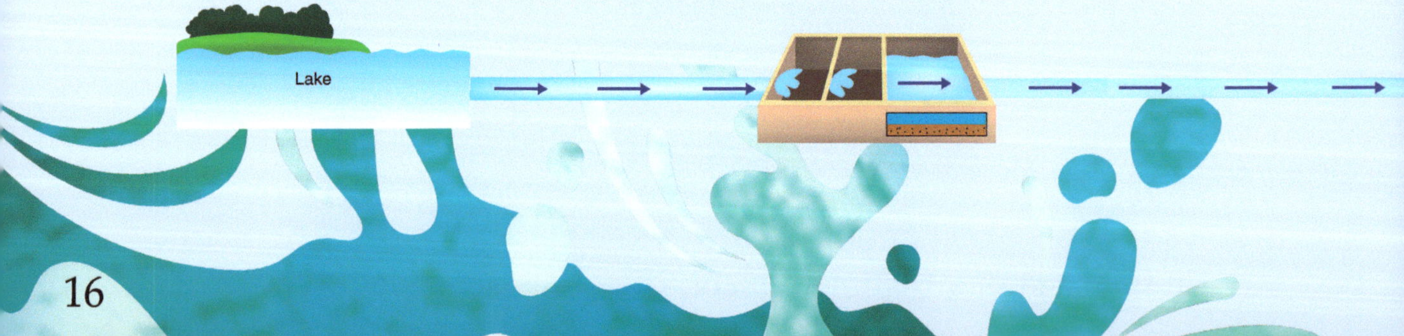

Water flows from storage tanks through underground pipes called mains. Large water mains connect to smaller pipes. These pipes carry clean water to homes, schools, and businesses.

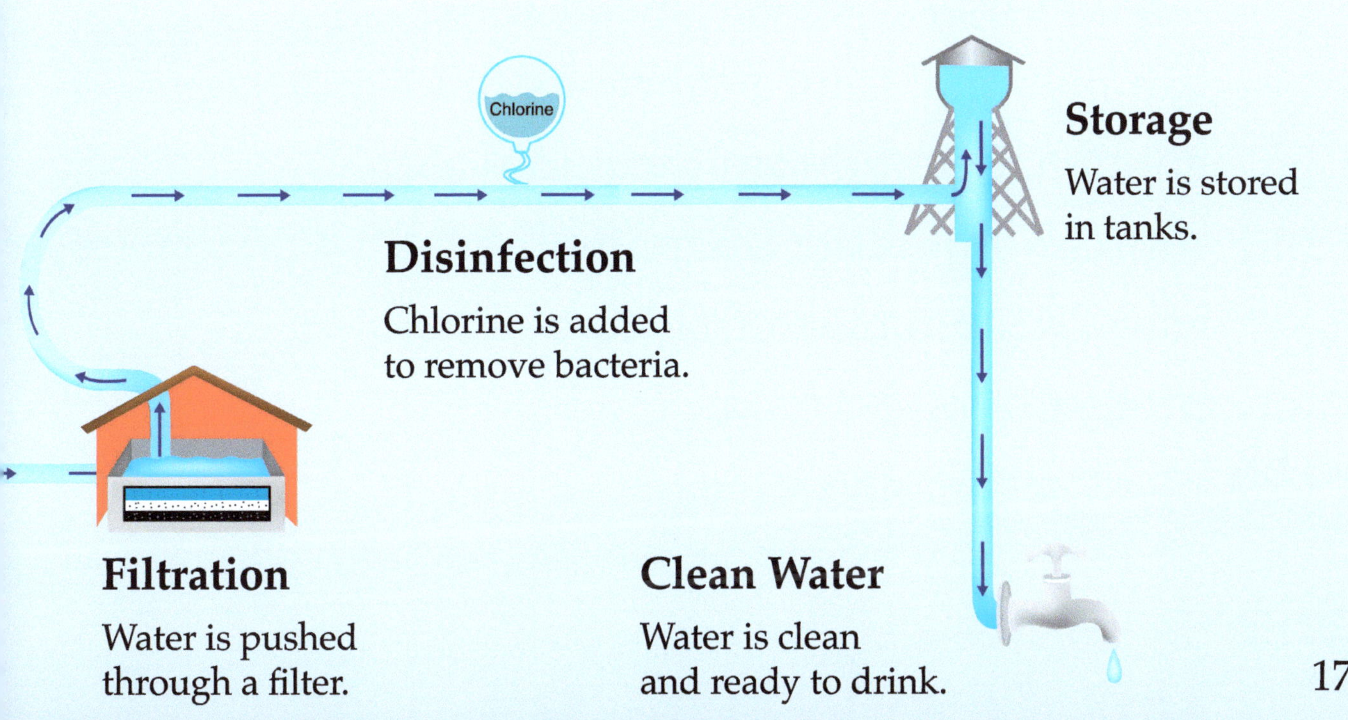

Clean Water

People need clean water to drink, cook, and bathe. In some parts of the world, people don't have enough clean water. Unclean water can cause illness.

Don't waste water. Saving water can help make sure everyone has enough. Don't dump trash in water sources or pollute them in other ways. Keeping water clean will help protect it for everyone.

Fact!
Every year 3.4 million
people die from diseases
caused by unclean
drinking water.

Amazing But True!

Plants help keep water clean. Some plants grow in wetlands. Particles stick to plant roots and settle into the dirt. Water is cleaned as it flows through layers of roots and dirt.

Hands On: Cleaning Water

Water treatment plants remove sediment from water with alum. This experiment will show you how alum works.

What You Need

- 1 cup (240 milliliters) cold water
- clear jar
- 1/2 teaspoon (1.25 grams) ground coffee
- 1 teaspoon (2.5 g) flour

What You Do

1. Pour the cold water into the clear jar.

2. Add the ground coffee.

3. Look at the jar. Notice how the coffee floats on top of the water.

4. Sprinkle the flour into the jar.

5. Look at the jar to see what happens. The flour will form little clumps. As the clumps get heavier, they fall to the bottom of the jar bringing coffee grounds with them. Alum works the same way in a water tank. Particles of dirt stick to the alum. The particles sink to the bottom of the tank.

Glossary

aquifer (AK-wuh-fuhr)—an underground lake

bacteria (bak-TIHR-ee-uh)—very small living things; some bacteria cause disease

chemical (KEM-uh-kuhl)—a substance that creates a reaction; chlorine is a chemical used to treat water

disinfection (dis-in-FEKT-shuhn)—a process that kills harmful germs

filter (FIL-tur)—a device that cleans liquids or gases as they pass through it

groundwater (GROUND-WAH-tur)—water that is found underground

particle (PAR-tuh-kuhl)—a tiny piece of something

pollute (puh-LOOT)—to make something dirty or unsafe

reservoir (REZ-ur-vwar)—an artificial lake where water is collected

sediment (SED-uh-muhnt)—bits of sand or clay carried by water or wind

toxin (TOK-sin)—poison

water treatment plant (WAH-tur TREET-muhnt PLANT)—a place where water is cleaned for people to use at home

Read More

Canavan, Roger. *You Wouldn't Want to Live without Clean Water!* You Wouldn't Want To. New York: Franklin Watts, 2015.

Mulder, Michelle. *Every Last Drop: Bringing Clean Water Home.* Victoria, Canada: Orca Book Publishers, 2014.

Oxlade, Chris. *Water.* How Does My Home Work? Chicago: Heinemann, 2013.

Internet Sites

FactHound offers a safe, fun way to find Internet sites related to this book. All of the sites on FactHound have been researched by our staff.

Here's all you do:

Visit *www.facthound.com*

Type in this code: 9781491482780

Check out projects, games and lots more at
www.capstonekids.com

Critical Thinking Using the Common Core

1. Why shouldn't people dump waste in water sources or pollute them in other ways? (Key Idea and Details)
2. What would happen if there were no water treatment plants on Earth? How would life be different for people? (Integration of Knowledge and Ideas)
3. Reread pages 6 and 7. Compare and contrast how water gets from wells to people's homes and how water gets from lakes and rivers to people's homes. (Craft and Structure)

Index